St. Augustine

Castillo de San Marcos National Monument is St. Augustine's most impressive historical landmark. It was begun by the Spanish in 1672, making it the oldest masonry fortification in what is now the United States. Castillo de San Marcos replaced nine earlier wooden defenses which had rotted away.

The stone used in the fort and in many of St. Augustine's colonial buildings is coquina, a shellrock formation which is quarried on Anastasia Island across the bay. Coquina is quite soft and porous in its natural state, but rapidly hardens when exposed to air. The large blocks were floated across the bay by barge, and then lifted into place by Indians and slaves using hand-operated derricks. The Castillo withstood two English sieges but was never captured by an enemy.

Fort Matanzas

The British siege of 1740 convinced Gov. Manuel de Montiano that he needed to have more than just a wooden tower at Matanzas Inlet, located 14 miles south of St. Augustine. If the British had been able to seize that point, they would probably have been able to starve the city into surrender. In 1742 Montiano ordered a strong, coquina tower to be built. It was well situated for defending St. Augustine's "back door". Fort Matanzas is now a National Monument.

St. Augustine Lighthouse

This beautiful black and white striped lighthouse on Anastasia Island is one of the most impressive stations in Florida. Completed in 1874, the present tower is St. Augustine's first and oldest surviving brick structure. It stands 165-feet tall and houses a first order Fresnel lens which casts a light that can be seen up to 20 miles out to sea. The 219 steps of the tower can be climbed for a breathtaking view of St. Augustine while the keepers' house has been restored to the year 1888.

City Gate at one time was the only entrance to the town. A moat ran from the Castillo westward to the San Sebastian River. A wall on the south side of the moat, known as the Cubo Defense Line protected the land approaches from the north. A drawbridge at this gate was raised each evening and not lowered until the following morning. The street that begins at the gate and runs south is Saint George Street.

St. George Street was the main street in early St. Augustine, beginning at the city gates. Reconstruction began in this area and continues to go on through the city. This is one of the most interesting streets in St. Augustine — this area was started in the 16th century.

12

Spanish Quarter Village This living history museum brings to life and explores the world of early colonists in a garrison town of 18th century Spanish Colonial Florida. Visit Señora Gallegos as she cooks a meal over a charcoal fire. Watch as the woodworker shapes handles and repairs furniture. Observe the blacksmith while he makes nails & wrought iron items!

Government House Museum The voyage continues with a visit to the museum of historic St. Augustine. Exhibits show the age of exploration of Florida's early years and the five centuries of St. Augustine's history from early native settlements, through European, to the turn of the Century.

The Old Market was a public market built in 1824 on a site that had public markets since 1598. There was a bell in the cupola to call villagers to market day when vegetables, meats, and fish were sold. The gabled roof was destroyed in the fire of 1887 and rebuilt by the townspeople.

The Oldest House

The González-Alvarez House, known to generations of tourists and townspeople as "The Oldest House," is one of the country's most studied and best-documented old houses. This National Historic Landmark is on a site believe to have been occupied since the early 1600s. Its walls date back to at least 1727. From its original walls, the house was expanded by its British and Territorial American owners. It is owned and operated by the St. Augustine Historical Society.

The Oldest Wooden School House

was erected in the 18th century. The professor and his family lived in the upstairs of the school house. The building served as a guard house and shelter for the city gate sentries during the Seminole War (1834-1841) since this was the closest unoccupied building to the city gate. The building was rented out in 1920 as a tea house and gift shop. In 1936 it opened on the same site as an historic exhibition building restored as the 1864 schoolroom and teacher's living quarters.

Mission of Nombre de Dios

Spanish explorer Pedro Menendez de Aviles, with soldiers, priests and colonists, landed here and founded St. Augustine, making it the oldest continually occupied European settlement in North America. On September 8, 1565, Father Francisco Lopez de Mendoza Grajales offered the first Mass in America's first city. Nombre de Dios is America's First Mission and our Lady of La Leche Shrine is America's Oldest Marian Shrine.

Ponce de Leon's
Fountain of Youth Park

Ponce de Leon came ashore to claim Florida for Spain in 1513. The Fountain of Youth Park exhibits exciting evidence of the early Timucuan Indian inhabitants

as well as evidence of the existence of sixteenth-century Spaniards. The site also has a navigator's celestial planetarium depicting astrological sailing techniques employed by Ponce de Leon. See and understand the life-style experienced by early Florida Indians, Spanish explorers and soldiers of fortune. You can drink from the pre-historic Indian Spring that Ponce de Leon hoped was the fabled Fountain of Youth.

Henry Morrison Flagler

During the winter of 1883-84 Henry M. Flagler, co-founder of Standard Oil Co., visited the city and was so impressed with the charm and possibilities of the area, he had two new hotels built, the Ponce de Leon in 1888 and the Alcazar in 1889. Flagler purchased the newly constructed Casa Monica and renamed it the Hotel Cordova. With the opening of these hotels, the wealthy and fashionable flocked to St. Augustine, which became known as the "Southern Newport." Flagler purchased the surrounding railroads creating the Florida East Coast Railway, which later extended all the way to Key West.

Ripley's Believe It or Not!

Located in historic "Castle Warden", a beautifully restored landmark, the museum of three floors has one-of-a-kind exhibits collected from around the world that will entertain and fascinate the entire family.

Alligator Farm

Explore the land of crocodiles, tropical birds, monkeys and many other exotic animals from around the world.

Memorial Presbyterian Church

The church was built by Henry M. Flagler in 1889 as a memorial to his only daughter, Jenny Louise Benedict, who died at sea in route to St. Augustine. It is a fine example of Venetian Renaissance architecture with a dome that is more than 100 feet in height. Henry Flagler and his daughter are buried in the mausoleum.

The Basilica-Cathedral

This church was begun in 1793, financed largely by the Spanish royal treasury, plus contributions of materials and labor on the part of the local citizens. The church was completed and dedicated in 1797 and became a cathedral in 1870. The bell tower and transept were added and interior remodeled after a fire in 1887 destroyed all but the exterior walls.

Grace United Methodist Church

Henry Flagler wanted the land occupied by the Olivet Methodist Church that sat on the proposed site for the Alcazar Hotel. In exchange for the land, Henry Flagler built a new church in 1887 on the corner of Carrera and Cordova Streets. It was designed by the architects of the Ponce de Leon Hotel.

The Trinity Episcopal Church

was the first Episcopal Church to be established in the state of Florida. The cornerstone was laid in 1825, and the building was enlarged in 1850, 1892 and 1902. The stained glass window in the chapel was done by Tiffany.

Bridge of Lions, with Mediterranean Revival towers, was built in 1926 to give autos access to Anastasia Island. The bridge is named for the two lion statues at the west end of bridge by sculptor Romanelli of Florence, Italy. They were donated by Dr. Andrew Anderson of St. Augustine.

St. Augustine
Visitor Information Center

Located on the corner of San Marco Ave. and Castillo Drive.
You can receive free information, maps, and an orientation movie
to help you make your stay in St. Augustine a pleasant one.